M000013879

CAN I SMOKE POT?

Marijuana in Light of Scripture

Tom Breeden and Mark L. Ward Jr.
Cruciform Press | October 2016

To faculty and friends at
Reformed Theological Seminary – Washington, DC,
who taught me to ask and answer the question:
"What does the Bible say?"

– Tom Breeden

To the many people I love on the West Side of
Greenville, South Carolina.

– Mark L. Ward, Jr.

CruciformPress

Table of Contents

Cruciform Press

Books of about 100 pages
Clear, inspiring, gospel-centered
CruciformPress.com

We like to keep it simple. So we publish short, clear, useful, inexpensive books for Christians and other curious people. Books that make sense and are easy to read, even as they tackle serious subjects.

We do this because the good news of Jesus Christ— the gospel—is the only thing that actually explains why this world is so wonderful and so awful all at the same time. Even better, the gospel applies to every single area of life, and offers real answers that aren't available from any other source.

These are books you can afford, enjoy, finish easily, benefit from, and remember. Check us out and see. Then join us as part of a publishing revolution that's good news for the gospel, the church, and the world.

Can I Smoke Pot? — Marijuana in Light of Scripture

Print / PDF ISBN: 978-1-941114-20-9
ePub ISBN: 978-1-941114-22-3
Mobipocket ISBN: 978-1-941114-21-6

MARIJUANA AND THE BIBLE
AN OPENING WORD

If you can't use the Bible to answer your questions, you don't really understand it.

The Bible contains all the divine words we need to know God, to please him, and to live righteous lives. Even if it doesn't always answer our specific questions, it does speak *in some way* to every aspect of life. Often it does this through general commands. For example, there are no situations in which it's okay to take part in "the unfruitful works of darkness" (Ephesians 5:11), no ways in which you can be "conformed to this world" (Romans 12:2), and no places where you can make "provision for the flesh" (Romans 13:14). No corner of human life is exempt from the norms in Scripture; we are to do "all to the glory of God" (1 Corinthians 10:31).

So can a Christian smoke pot for God's glory?

Just search the Bible for the word *marijuana*. You'll strike out. Search for any verse containing

weed, dank, green, 420, herb, ganja, Mary Jane—
nothing. (Look for *pot* and you will, admittedly, get
a bunch of search results, but not very helpful ones in
this case.)

But questions about pot won't go away, so how
do we get answers from a Christian perspective?

Christians get answers on fundamentally moral
questions from the Bible. And if you can't use the
Bible to answer a moral question with reasonable
clarity, you're misunderstanding it somewhere. You
need some help using it.

Good and Necessary Consequence

The students and teachers of the Bible who put
together the classic and influential *Westminster Confession of Faith* were not faced with a societal debate
over medical and recreational marijuana use, but
they did encounter equally pressing moral issues to
which the Bible did not speak directly.

Four-hundred years ago, they saw that
sometimes we have to answer our moral questions
"by good and necessary consequence" from what
the Bible says more generally.[1] We have to interpret
Scripture. A few quick examples:

- The Bible never explicitly says that porn videos
  are wrong, but this conclusion is a good and

necessary consequence of Jesus' statement that "everyone who looks at a woman with lustful intent has already committed adultery with her in his heart" (Matthew 5:28).

- The Bible never specifically says that downloading pirated music and movies is wrong (although *pirate* should be a clue), but this conclusion is a good and necessary consequence of the commandment not to steal (Exodus 20:15).
- The Bible never says what the alternative minimum tax rate should be, or which public lands should permit logging, or how many shoes a person should own—and even when answers to these questions are appropriately different in different situations, the Bible sets the boundaries inside which these moral decisions must be made.

In short, the Bible sets out for us the system of values *without which* we cannot make God-pleasing choices in the first place.

So if you're looking for explicit passages about marijuana in the Bible, you'll be disappointed. They aren't there. And yet the Bible isn't silent. The goal of this book is to provide the basic theological framework, built directly on biblical statements, that you will need to answer your questions about marijuana to the glory of God. (And if you'd like some more guidance on how to get answers from Scripture in general, check out the Appendix.)

One
MARIJUANA AND CREATION

In the beginning, God created pot.

Every Christian discussion of marijuana, or of anything in creation, has to begin there, where the Bible does. In the first verse of the first chapter of the first book of the Bible, the book of Genesis, *Creator* is the way God chooses to introduce himself to the world. Before we find out that God exists in Trinity or that he is love—and long before we find out that just because God created something doesn't necessarily mean you should put it in your mouth—we learn that God is Creator.

Christians generally consider the author of Genesis to be Moses. In his day, the gods with the highest public-approval ratings made the world by accident in a fight, or out of a lazy desire for slave labor. But in the account that Moses presents, God creates and fills the world methodically, carefully. The creation is, consequently, like its creator: it is "good" (Genesis 1:4; 1:10; 1:12; 1:18; 1:21; 1:25), even "very good" (Genesis 1:31).

The speech of God in Genesis culminates with his speaking into existence the highest and best of his creations, the only creation to bear his image and likeness: man and woman. "Let us make man in our image," God said. And it was so.

That is how man, marijuana, and everything else came to be. And all of it was good.

Fall: Sin Infects Creation

As everyone who's made it at least a few days into a Bible-reading plan knows, however, the perfect goodness of creation didn't last. Sin slinks into the story of the Bible, and into the cosmos, by page 3. Instead of embracing the goodness of creation, Adam and Eve choose to rebel against God. And they jump into this rebellion with all four feet then in existence. Adam and Eve, given kingly and queenly rule over God's creation, led the world into futility and ruin. At that first sin, all of creation enters what Christians call the fall.

The good gift of children will now be painful, and the good gift of marriage will be disordered (Genesis 3:16). The natural world will bring pain to humanity (3:17-18). The good gifts of working, keeping, having dominion, and subduing will become frustrating and difficult (3:19).

But the inherent goodness of creation will not go away: wombs will still bear children, marriages will still bring genuine happiness, and plants will still grow. The fall marred God's good creation but did not destroy it. Creation is still good, but because of the curse it is now marked with a futility and corruption that were not part of its original state.

And fallen creation is still beautiful. Even after sin brings a curse upon God's world, the Bible continues to treat the splendor of creation as a reason for God to be worshipped. Creation puts man in his place, both humbling him and exalting him:

> When I look at your heavens, the work of your fingers,
> the moon and the stars, which you have set in place,
> what is man that you are mindful of him,
> and the son of man that you care for him? (Psalm 8:3-4)

Creation, even after the fall, declares God's glory to all people:

> The heavens declare the glory of God,
> and the sky above proclaims his handiwork. (Psalm 19:1)

Mankind itself, standing tallest and therefore falling furthest, is still a source of wonder:

> For you formed my inward parts;
> you knitted me together in my mother's womb.
> I praise you, for I am fearfully and wonderfully
> made. (Psalm 139:13-14)

Redemption: New Testament, New Creation

The New Testament ushers in something entirely wonderful—a new act of creation. This is a redemption promised even in the Garden of Eden (Genesis 3:15) and echoed repeatedly throughout the Old Testament (Isaiah 65:17-25; Jeremiah 31:31-40; Ezekiel 36:33-36). It breaks into this fallen world through the person and work of Jesus, the Son of God, the Second Person of the Trinity.

When the Bible speaks of this new creation, however, we must not think of God tossing the old creation in the cosmic trash bin, dusting off his hands, and starting over.[2] No, the new creation taking place *after* the fall, as one theologian has illustrated it, is like a child who contracts a life-threatening disease.[3] He still grows, he is still irreplaceable—his parents would be rightly offended at a doctor's suggestion that they just get a new kid. But he is not all he was meant to be.

12

New creation, in this illustration, is like a cure that comes along for the boy's disease at some point after the diagnosis. The cure enables him to get back onto the fully healthy path of growth he was meant to be on. Sometime later, thanks to the cure there is little trace of the disease left in him.

The new creation is therefore the fulfillment of creation's original intent. However, as theologian John Frame says, it's not as if the new creation was a:

> "Plan B" to replace an original creation that God had somehow failed to keep on course. Redemption was God's plan before the creation of the world (1 Corinthians 2:7; Ephesians 1:5-11; 2 Timothy 1:9; Titus 1:2). The new creation represents the *telos*, the goal, of the old.[4]

After all, we Christians are ourselves "new creations" — everyone in Christ is (2 Corinthians 5:17) — yet at no point does God completely start over with us. We remain ourselves even after we become new creations in Christ.

Romans 8 is the key New Testament passage explaining how creation, Fall, and redemption all come together in a truly biblical theology.[5] It suggests that the scope of Christ's redemptive work is as great as the scope of the fall.

The creation waits with eager longing for the revealing of the sons of God. For the creation was subjected to futility, not willingly, but because of him who subjected it, in hope that the creation itself will be set free from its bondage to corruption and obtain the freedom of the glory of the children of God. For we know that the whole creation has been groaning together in the pains of childbirth until now. And not only the creation, but we ourselves, who have the firstfruits of the Spirit, groan inwardly as we wait eagerly for adoption as sons, the redemption of our bodies. (Romans 8:19-23)

Creation is not accomplishing everything it was designed to do; it has been "subjected to futility." But at the "revealing of the sons of God" — when the children of God are revealed in glory at the return of Jesus Christ — so too will creation be glorified. When Christians receive their fully resurrected, glorious bodies on the last day, creation itself will be set free from futility and attain that same glory. The new creation is not a replacement. It is a restoration.

Every time someone becomes a believer in Christ, or even when a Christian simply obeys his or her Lord, an act of partial but meaningful restoration has occurred. At that moment of obedience, the rule of Christ is breaking into the world, hinting at (and sometimes shouting) what re-creation will one day look like. We are taught to pray, "Thy kingdom come." And it will. And it has.

Only when Christ returns will God's restorative work be complete. Then we will enjoy what John saw at the Bible's close: "a new heaven and a new earth." We'll see God take his dwelling place with man. "They will be his people, and God himself will be with them as their God." All tears, mourning, pain—all the "former things" brought by Adam and Eve's sin will have passed away (Revelation 21:1–4).

The Bible is the story of what God is doing to glorify himself by redeeming his fallen creation. One day, he will remove the curse completely and restore the world to the way he created it to be.

Creation and Marijuana

A good creation means that created things are good. Creation is not neutral; it's good. It's not merely potentially good; it's good. The actual, tangible *stuff* of creation is good. Pot is good. The coca plant is good. Tobacco is good. Hops are good.

And yet, influenced heavily by Greek philosophy, many early Christians believed precisely that the material world is bad and only the *spiritual* world is good. Still today there are Christians who are nervous or suspicious about the goodness of created things—such as emotions, or authority, or the body.

A Christian college student once pinched the skin on his arm and said to his friend, "Flesh—this stuff is bad, right?" A young seminarian approached his theology professor for counsel about his poor health, and was upset when he was told to get sufficient sleep and stop eating so much junk food. "Someday I'll be rid of this body, so why should I care so much about it now?" the student said. He was expecting more "spiritual" counsel.

If the body is bad, then why did God call it good? Adam had flesh, didn't he? And if it's temporary, why does Jesus still have a physical body at this moment? (1 Corinthians 15:22-23).

Everything God made is good *for its intended purpose(s)*. An ascetic rejection of God's good creation—a refusal to enjoy, or let others enjoy, the good things God has made—is what Paul calls a "doctrine of devils" (1 Timothy 4:1–4 KJV). Make no mistake: Christianity is about our whole being, body and spirit. Because God created everything, it is *all* his concern.

Marijuana is Good

If we don't start our discussion of marijuana by rightly pointing out that it's good, we may begin to blame God for any bad uses to which it's put. If *Cannabis sativa* is inherently evil, and God created it, what else could we conclude?[6]

What's so good about marijuana, then? What possible good reason could God have for creating something that you can smoke or ingest to get high?

There are answers to this question, and we'll get into them later. But right now we have to make an important distinction before we talk about medical and recreational uses of pot: there is a major difference between saying *there must be good purposes for marijuana* and saying that *all purposes of marijuana must be good.*

Fire is used for cooking and for warmth. But fire has also been used to destroy via arson, and to murder via Molech. Fire is good, but not every use humans make of it is good. Fire is good, but (unless you work for a circus) that doesn't mean you should put it in your mouth.

God created uranium, too; it isn't a doctrine of devils to forbid people to sprinkle it on their ice cream.

Respectable, buttoned-down, middle-class, church-attending Western Christians need to say full-throatedly that marijuana is good — or they'll be betraying Genesis 1 and 2. For reasons of deep biblical-theological principle, we must enter this discussion about marijuana looking not just for the wicked ways marijuana can be used, but the good ones. We were given dominion "over all the earth" by our creator, and told to subdue it — that is, pushing it towards its full potential and maximizing its usefulness for mankind. It would be wrong to exclude even one plant from the morally good category we call creation.

That said, now we must be ready to address the next logical question: OK, marijuana is good, but *good for what*?

Takeaways for Chapter 1

1. God created the world good, including the stuff of creation. Marijuana is good.
2. The curse of sin affects all of creation. Creation retains its goodness, but it falls short of the full goodness for which it was designed.
3. Just because a created thing is good does not mean that all uses of that created thing are good, too.

Two

MARIJUANA AND GOVERNMENT

So God created pot, and he created it good. And yet...before we can even consider the controversial uses of cannabis—the proposed medical and recreational uses—we have to talk about a few other things God created that are relevant to our moral choices: our neighbors.

None of us are moral free-agents. Our lives are affected by the opinions of others. This is because, in the chain of authority that helps hold society together, there are generally people above, beside, and below us, all of whom have some claims on our moral decisions. Rarely, in the structured world God made, is God the only authority with whom we must deal. He gave us a social world: parental, spousal, business, governmental, and other authorities have various God-given rights to speak into our choices. Therefore, if we want to make any claim to living rightly or honorably or respectfully or responsibly in the world God has made, we cannot decide to smoke marijuana without taking others into account.

Two quick examples:

- If a parent instructs you not to smoke marijuana, you have a moral obligation to obey. Why? Because God gives parents to children as an extension (however imperfect) of his authority over all creation, and over people in particular. Even if you don't live in your parent's home, and no matter your age or degree of independence, God still calls you to give serious consideration to any guidance you receive from a parent.[7] Even evil fathers know how to give good gifts to their children, Jesus said (Matthew 7:11), and one of those gifts is often a healthy caution rooted in experiences parents wish they hadn't had.
- If God has placed you under employers or other authority figures (pastors, teachers, mentors) who discourage the recreational or medical use of marijuana, the Bible's default counsel is that you honor such people. They will give an account for their leadership over you; make sure they do it with joy and not grief (Hebrews 13:17).

The rest of this chapter will focus on the one human authority that possesses the God-given power—the long arm—necessary to threaten truly serious consequences (or offer significant incentives) to those who cultivate or use certain mind-altering substances. That authority is, of course, government. We need to talk about its role in the debate over marijuana before we dig into the real controversy.

Government in the Old Testament

God planted the seed of all human government in Eden, before you might have thought it was needed. That seed rises out of the *dominion*—a kingly word— God delegated to mankind when they were created. Government, too, is a good created thing.

Creation and Government

The dominion God invested in Adam and Eve in Genesis 1:26–28 was far-reaching. Adam and Eve were told to "fill" and "subdue" and "have dominion over" not just their garden, but "all the earth." We were also told to "work" and "keep"—that is, to develop and preserve—the sectors of creation under our individual care. This is called the creation mandate or the dominion mandate, and it is good.

Humanity was created to be God's representative authority, a major means by which he exerts his rule on our planet. It's important to notice that this authority was given to us before the fall, and that the

Bible never repeals this authority. We are blessed and we are mandated to fill, subdue, and rule.

Even if the fall had never happened, human government would have been a necessary part of mankind's filling, subduing, and ruling operation. *Government*, after all, is simply the name we give to an organized group of people to whom a given community has granted authority to ensure justice and promote fairness. Somebody has to view agricultural water usage from the perspective of all the inhabitants in the river valley, and not just of those in a particular town. Somebody has to levy the tax necessary for the upkeep of the road the whole valley uses, or that connects them with another valley.

Government, in other words, is a God-created good. As soon as people attempt seriously to live out the blessing of the creation mandate on any scale larger than an individual family, they will need government. Government is not a concession to human sin, but part of God's design.

The Fall and Government
But of course sin did enter the world, and human government has had to adjust to this terrible reality. In particular, God gives government the power of the "sword" (Romans 13:4), the sole right to exercise divinely sanctioned violence. God tells Noah as he leaves the ark,

> And for your lifeblood I will require a reckoning:
> from every beast of the field I will require it and
> from man. From his fellow man I will require a
> reckoning for the life of man.
>
> Whoever sheds the blood of man,
> By man shall his blood be shed,
> For God made man in his own image. (Genesis
> 9:5-6)

Beings who bear the divine image have inestimable worth. Therefore, when any creature treats other men like so much garbage to be thrown out, a payment must be exacted in the form of punishment. God will not permit people to destroy his picture—each time, a price must be paid to display and affirm the abiding value of God's image.

God doesn't always use government as a middleman to deal with human sin. Sometimes he acts directly. He sent fire to consume Nadab and Abihu (Leviticus 10:1-2), and he swallowed up into the ground Dathan and Abiram (Numbers 16). But it is important to note that, generally speaking, God doesn't wield the sword in his own hand but places it in the hands of mere humans—even after the fall. If a man sheds blood, by *man* shall his blood be shed.

Wayne Grudem draws an important inference from Genesis 9:5–6:

No further details are given here regarding civil government. But in speaking these words to Noah, God establishes the obligation to carry out the most severe punishment (the taking of human life) in retribution for the most horrible crime (the murder of another human being). Once this principle is established, then the imposition of lesser penalties for lesser crimes is also validated, since if a government has the right to carry out the most severe kind of punishment, then it certainly has the right to carry out lesser punishments for lesser crimes as well.[8]

Other portions of Scripture also point to the value and scope of human government in a fallen world. The book of Judges describes how Israel's lack of a king resulted in chaos. Throughout history, nations without leadership have inevitably moved rapidly toward just the kind of right-in-their-own-eyes anarchy—both societal, religious, and sexual—that ancient Israel did. Government exists in part to restrain evil. It constitutes a major portion of the "common grace" God shows to mankind.[9]

It's true that most of Israel's kings turned out to be awful rulers. Even so, this does not call into question the intrinsic value of human government. It simply displays what happens when government acts dishonorably—in short, as an autonomous authority rather than as a divinely delegated one. The ideal king described by Deuteronomy 17:14-20 is one who is submissive to God's word—to the point that he actually copies it all out by hand! Failed governments, including many of those Israelite kings, illustrate what happens, not when there is no king, but when *kings* act as if there is no *King*.

Government in the New Testament

The church and the nation of Israel are not the same thing. It's not generally wise to draw a direct line from the government of ancient Israel to the American government—or the French, Chinese, Djiboutian, or any other government. We know this because the Bible tells us so.

In the Old Testament, religion and government formed one institution, not two. This is why the Pentateuch, the first five books of the Bible, pre-scribes *civil* punishments for *religious* violations. But in the New Testament, many of the laws that the Old Testament spends so much time explaining are specifically repealed. In one seemingly off-hand action, Jesus "declared all foods clean" (Mark 7:19), thus overturning scores of regulations that the Isra-elites had been required to observe meticulously for thousands of years.

God did not alter his method of rule on a whim,

but for the best possible reason—Jesus perfectly fulfilled all the Old Testament laws in order to set up a new and better system. In the Old Testament, God expressed his rule through a single theocratic nation. After the institution of the New Covenant in and through Jesus Christ, people from *every* kindred, tribe, people, and nation are invited to submit to God's rule—without leaving their tribes, their nations, or their governments. Unlike the Old Testament, the New Testament places religion and government in separate spheres.

Far from undermining the power and authority of human government, the New Testament insists in the most definite way that obedience to human government is an important part of Christian discipleship. With one brilliant epigram, "Render to Caesar the things that are Caesar's, and to God the things that are God's" (Matthew 22:21), Jesus supports the right of (even) pagan governments to tax, and the responsibility of (especially) believing citizens to pay.

Paul is less poetic, but just as definite. He not only commands that Christians obey the relevant government authorities, he actually calls government officials "ministers of God" (Romans 13:6). Yes, there are times when Christians must choose to "obey God rather than men" (Acts 5:29), times when governmental authority conflicts directly with divine authority. But the default expectation of the

New Testament is that governments are good institutions that promote good in society:

> Let every person be subject to the governing
> authorities. For there is no authority except from
> God, and those that exist have been instituted
> by God. ²Therefore whoever resists the authori-
> ties resists what God has appointed, and those
> who resist will incur judgment. ³ For rulers are
> not a terror to good conduct, but to bad. Would
> you have no fear of the one who is in authority?
> Then do what is good, and you will receive his
> approval, ⁴ for he is God's servant for your good.
> But if you do wrong, be afraid, for he does not
> bear the sword in vain. For he is the servant of
> God, an avenger who carries out God's wrath
> on the wrongdoer. ⁵ Therefore one must be in
> subjection, not only to avoid God's wrath but
> also for the sake of conscience. ⁶ For because of
> this you also pay taxes, for the authorities are
> ministers of God, attending to this very thing. ⁷
> Pay to all what is owed to them: taxes to whom
> taxes are owed, revenue to whom revenue is
> owed, respect to whom respect is owed, honor
> to whom honor is owed. (Romans 13:1-7)

The government as Paul sees it (by divine inspi-
ration) is not merely a promoter of good. It is an

"avenger" of evil. And the punishment it metes out to "wrongdoers" is actually an expression of God's "wrath" (vv 4-5)! As a general rule, resisting the government is *the same as* resisting God (v 2).

Peter also joins Paul (and Jesus) in upholding the divinely delegated authority of human government in the New Covenant era. In 1 Peter 2:13-17, Peter hits the same themes Paul did: believers are to "be subject" to "emperors" as well as "governors." And governors are actually supposed to "punish those who do evil" as well as "praise those who do good." Peter then issues a command which, if followed today by professing Christians, would require the removal of an awful lot of bumper stickers: Peter simply wrote, "Honor the emperor."

So we see that the New Testament modulates but affirms the Old Testament teaching that human government is ordained by God and should be honored. If anything, the modulation is into a higher key: even when governments are not theocratic, we are told to obey, and governors are told to promote good and curb evil. Government is a God-created good with definite God-given tasks in this fallen world.

Government and the Influence of Sin

Of course, human governments don't always live up to the norms provided for them in the New

Testament. Their job of fighting the effects of the fall and encouraging the good in creation is complicated by the fact that governments are *themselves* twisted by the fall—and run by fallen people. There is no perfect governmental system in this fallen world because there are no perfect people.

Governments regularly fail to punish evil, perhaps especially when that evil is found within the government itself. Governments also misidentify good and evil, switching the labels, as it were. The very worst injustices in the world are often those committed by government, precisely because such great power has been placed in its hands. Swords kill, and so do governments of every political persuasion.

Peter and Paul, remember, were living under the same government that had executed the Lord Jesus Christ himself. They were not naïve. They knew that governments sometimes send soldiers to kill 2-year-olds (Matthew 2:16), and sometimes mix the blood of innocent religious pilgrims with their sacrifices (Luke 13:1).

So, how should Christians respond to human government when it is clearly in the wrong?

New Testament scholar Douglas Moo points Christians back to the opening words of Romans 13 for help in answering this question. He sees significance in Paul's choice of one word in particular: *submit*. Christians aren't supposed to merely comply.

When it comes to obeying government, we aren't called to just go through the motions begrudgingly because life is simpler that way. We are called to *submit*, and true submission begins in the heart.

Our external obedience to authority is meant to reflect an internal acknowledgment that government is ultimately God-ordained, and therefore we willingly place ourselves under its rule. Yes, if we believe certain laws are wrong before God, we should speak and act in ways intended to bring change. However, as Moo says, "To submit is to recognize one's subordinate place in a hierarchy, to acknowledge as a general rule that certain people or institutions have 'authority' over us."[10]

That hierarchy rises all the way to God himself, and every "power" in it draws its power (and right) from that ultimate source. Only when government very clearly rebels against God, stepping completely out of the line of hierarchy that give it its power (and right), do Christians have any power (or right) to resist it.

Government and Marijuana

Given our discussion in this chapter, one basic conclusion seems inescapable. If any civil government says that its citizens can't smoke (or grow or sell or transport or eat or otherwise consume) marijuana or THC (its psychoactive ingredient), Christians are called by God to submit—unless they can find sufficient scriptural data justifying their disobedience. That's why this whole book (at least, in one sense and for certain readers) is completely unnecessary.

After all, Christians don't write books designed to help other Christians think through whether or not they should steal cars, visit prostitutes, engage in insider trading, or poison the neighbor's noisy dog. Clearly, the reasons this book exists and the reasons you are reading it are the same. First, Western nations are in the process of reconsidering and recategorizing marijuana use. Second, as the cultural climate shifts in favor of smoking pot, some Christians are honestly beginning to wonder why that's such a bad thing.

Indeed, in the United States in particular the legal situation with regard to marijuana use is increasingly complicated. There are states which have ruled it's legal to smoke pot simply because you want to (recreational use), and many more in which that remains illegal. But at this point in history, not even a state law permitting recreational use of marijuana may be seen by Christians as decisive—because at the federal level, it is still illegal! Even though the U.S. government has been inconsistent (to put it mildly) in the *enforcement* of its own laws in this area, marijuana is nevertheless a Schedule 1 controlled substance at the federal level, technically a no-no for practically all Americans, regardless of what state laws might say.[11]

It is certainly possible that the federal government will before too long decriminalize the recreational use of marijuana. After all, America winks at drunkenness and so highly values individual autonomy that this wouldn't be too surprising. But it must be noted that even if the President one day signs a bill to that effect, Christians living in any state that forbids recreational pot use are still forbidden by Scripture from indulging. Wherever Caesar speaks out of both sides of his mouth on this question, only one group will surely be safe: the abstainers. As of this writing, for any Christian, anywhere in the United States, to smoke pot is to resist the governing authorities. It is, in unmistakable terms, to resist God.

What about First Timothy 4?

So with human government being ordained by God, it appears that wherever government forbids the recreational use of pot, Christians are barred from doing so. Even if you really want to. And even if everybody else is doing it. But we do need to ask one more question: what about Paul's point in 1 Timothy 4:1-5?

Now the Spirit expressly says that in later times some will depart from the faith by devoting themselves to deceitful spirits and teachings of demons, through the insincerity of liars whose consciences are seared, who forbid marriage and require abstinence from foods that God created to be received with thanksgiving by those who believe and know the truth. For *everything created by God is good, and nothing is to be rejected if it is received with thanksgiving,* for it is made holy by the word of God and prayer. (1 Timothy 4:1-5)

Paul is speaking here of mistaken *religious* teaching, but the same basic question could be asked about government: what right does anyone have to tell someone else not to do something God calls good (such as getting married) or consume something that God calls good? Satan didn't create marriage or marijuana—God did, and he created them for specific good purposes—but Paul says that Satan did influence some "teachings" that can keep people away from good things like these. What if the U.S. government outlawed peanut butter?

Does this passage suggest that government may be out of line in outlawing marijuana? After all, THC, the active ingredient in marijuana, does seem to help some people with certain medical conditions, and lots of people draw parallels between pot and alcohol, noting that the Bible does leave room for moderate drinking. Are either or both of these "good" uses of pot that government *should* allow? We will specifically address these very important questions in later chapters. For now, let's focus on what Paul is saying about these false teachers.

Pretend for a moment that the teachers in 1 Timothy 4 are saying that Christians shouldn't eat a certain kind of berry. They don't appear to be saying, "Don't eat those berries; they'll make you *sick*." They're saying, "Don't eat berries; they're *wicked*." How do we know this? Because of Paul's replies to these "teachings of demons." His response is not to insist that the foods are *healthy* but instead to note, twice, that the foods they're forbidding are *created things*. Paul insists that "everything created by God is good."

Here, Paul obviously means good *for its intended purpose*. For example, many plants may have some nutritional value, but no one would argue they are all among the "foods that God created to be received with thanksgiving." (How about a few toxic mushrooms and some nice, fresh poison ivy in that salad?) So, based on what Paul is saying here, before you can ever ask whether government is out of bounds in outlawing marijuana, you have to ask the question we have already posed, the question this book will continue to explore: what is marijuana *good for*? Only where government forbids us to use something in the way God intended may we even begin to consider the possibility that government could be out of line in that area.

The Powers That Be

As we close out this chapter, recall for a moment the subtitle of this book: *Marijuana in Light of Scripture*. Our goal as authors is to give you our best, short reading of what the Bible says on this topic, completely apart from any personal preferences. When we speak unambiguously on a particular point, therefore, it's only because the Bible seems to speak that way.

Recall also that this chapter has a narrow focus. It examines one question: What is the role of government in determining whether someone is permitted, biblically, to "use" marijuana, whether medically or recreationally? Our answer: If government forbids marijuana use, don't use it. The government is God's minister to you for good. Thus, if any level of government under which you live outlaws marijuana use, you are not permitted by Scripture to break that law.

But we must also add that, even if all levels of government over you permit marijuana usage, there are still other people who have some right over your opinions and practice—including God. Thankfully, with the continued help of Scripture it is possible to gain some understanding of God's view of marijuana use. That's why you need to keep reading this book through to the end.

Takeaways for Chapter 2

1. Government is the system of authority that orders and regulates a society toward justice and the common good.

2. God created government for our good. It is one of the ways that he punishes evil and rewards good.

3. Because of the fall, human governments are not perfect. Sometimes they make incorrect or even wicked decisions. This doesn't mean we throw government out altogether.

4. Christians must submit the government in reverence to God unless government directly and explicitly contradicts his authority. God has placed governmental authorities over us.

Three
MARIJUANA AND MEDICINE

This is a book of Christian basics, so let's review.

- Chapter 1: God created the marijuana plant, so it's good. But because of the fall, not all *uses* of it are good.
- Chapter 2: God created government, too, as a legitimate although fallen and imperfect extension of his divine rule. Right now, very few governments anywhere in the world have legalized recreational or even medicinal uses of cannabis. And the Bible says obey your government.

In some ways, this chapter will walk a less certain line than chapters one and two, across some very personal territory. *After all*, we may be tempted to think, *what business does the government have telling us we can't use cannabis for its medicinal prop-*

*erties? If my child is having epileptic seizures, and if
cannabis can decrease them or their severity, what's
the bigger sin—disobeying the government or letting
my child suffer?*

Imagine this, because if it hasn't happened
quite this way yet, it soon will: a picture-perfect
Christian couple with beautiful children is suddenly
thrust into the crucible when their infant daughter
begins having seizures. The Christian community
mobilizes to pray for this little girl, people bring
meals, and a long line of doctors march in and out
of the ordeal to offer an equally long string of ultimately unhelpful opinions and treatments. Still the
little girl suffers.

Months pass. A year. Two years. No change.

And then this Christian mother, a Bible memory
champion who in high school recited the entire book
of First Corinthians, jot and tittle, begins to post
things on Facebook that alarm many in her conserva-
tive Christian community. She writes openly about
her desire to seek a new treatment for her daughter:
the medical use of cannabis. Her friends don't know
what to say. Who wants to tell a young mom with a
beautiful but desperately ill child, "Sometimes there
is no righteous way to mitigate suffering"?

Would you give her that counsel? Would you tell
her that because marijuana is most commonly used
for getting high, there is no way to use it righteously

and beneficially, so she must not even *try*? Could you back that up with Scripture?

Martin Lee, in his journalistically comprehensive book, *Smoke Signals*, cites study after anecdote after argument after doctor reputedly showing that marijuana is beneficial for all sorts of medical purposes.[12] Childhood chemo patients who eat THC-laced brownies stop vomiting. Adults with various painful disorders get some peace. It's not widely known, but the federal government even has a pot farm where medical-grade cannabis is grown for Americans who have pushed the legal system long and hard enough to obtain a court order granting them the liberty to use cannabis to treat their difficult medical conditions.

The daughter with the seizures, and the adults who've obtained court orders—if THC can possibly help them, this may be understandable for many of us. But then the question becomes: if it's okay for them, why not for everyone holding a doctor's prescription? If doctors are allowed to prescribe highly addictive opioids that can kill you if take a few pills too many, why couldn't they prescribe medical marijuana?

Useful vs. Permissible

Those questions are posed just to set the stage for this chapter. The authors don't want to make claims or arguments that rightly belong to physicians and medical researchers. Because the truth is that even if some form of cannabis treatment appeared to work for you, you are just one data point, an insufficient sample. Plus, you almost certainly failed to use the kind of rigorous empirical methodology that could rule out other causes for your improved health: perhaps it was the change of seasons; perhaps it was the placebo effect; perhaps your improvement would have happened without cannabis. Indeed, perhaps cannabis actually slowed a recovery that was developing for completely unrelated reasons.

These questions cannot be addressed in a book of this size, even if the authors felt they were up to the task. This book (and this chapter in particular) will focus not on whether marijuana is *useful* but whether it is *permissible*. That is: could pot (or any of its compounds) count as a medicine?

Medicine and the Bible

Christians have thought about medicine and the Bible before, going back to the time of the New Testament. Though some Christians have been—and still are today—skeptical of the power of medicine (particularly if there is money to be made by those who sell or administer the medicine), the consistent Christian position has been that wisely administering foreign substances to the body to promote healing is good, not bad. It mitigates the effects of the fall in a way consistent with God's word.

Christians take medicine because God works many of his divine purposes, including healing, through ordinary means. That is, he could use special power-zaps from faith healers; he could use pilgrimages to Lourdes; he could use a bronze serpent stuck up on a pole (and he did: see Numbers 21:8-9). But just as our skin heals itself through a process God built into it, so God typically uses methods that appear ordinary and routine to us, but are no less acts of God.

Medicine in the Old Testament

The Old Testament is full of healing, although references to medicine are scarce. The rapid expansion and development of modern medicine is the result of generations of scientific work — of living out the creation mandate of Genesis 1:26-28. Obviously, the great majority of medical treatments we use today were unavailable in ancient times. But the ancient world did have medicine. Balms, ointments, and oils — medical products derived from plants — appear throughout the Old Testament. Alcohol (likewise derived from plants) also had some medicinal uses. It is from these ancient treatments that we can develop our larger theology of medicine in the Old Testament.

Palliative Care in Proverbs 31

Proverbs 31:6 offers one example of God working through medical means:

> Give strong drink to the one who is perishing,
> and wine to those in bitter distress. (Proverbs
> 31:6)

This is palliative care—medicine administered for the sole purpose of making someone feel better temporarily, without actually promoting healing in any direct way. In fact, we have every reason to think that Proverbs 31:6 uses *perishing* quite literally. Someone is dying, and whatever is killing him or her is also causing great misery. This passage commends placing something foreign into the body—a strong alcoholic drink—to help alleviate that suffering.

This kind of distress can also be a valid reason for palliative care. *Bitter* is a severe term, one Naomi uses in the book of Ruth after losing her husband, her sons, her home, and life as she knew it (Ruth 1:20). It is important for us to note that this passage from Proverbs is found in the Bible's wisdom literature, a genre of Scripture which is not merely descriptive of a wise life but *prescriptive*. Palliative care of this sort is not just permissible, it is commendable.

Nonetheless, wisdom literature recognizes that different situations call for different applications of the one wisdom of God. Sometimes you answer a fool; sometimes you stay silent (Proverbs 26:4–5). Proverbs 31:6 does not stand all by itself. Even with Proverbs, there are counterbalancing statements about alcohol (more on this in the next chapter). The mother of King Lemuel, who taught him the wisdom of Proverbs 31, also instructed her son not to drink at all—precisely because kings must not be permitted to forget their troubles. Their troubles are the nation's troubles, and they are called to serve without mental impairment (Proverbs 31:4–5).

So Lemuel's mother is not inviting people of all ages to drink their troubles away. Drunkenness is condemned throughout the Bible: "Wine is a mocker, strong drink a brawler, and whoever is led astray by it is not wise" (Proverbs 20:1). The wise person weighs the statements of Scripture and applies them to his or her particular situation.

Looked at through lenses shaped by modern medical knowledge, the Bible appears to validate some use of prescription painkillers—we are to extend the mercy of God to those who suffer. One of the good values of created things after the fall is the medical properties they have. God can work his healing purposes through such means.

Hezekiah's Healing and the Asa Objection

Another example of God working his purposes

through ordinary means occurs in Isaiah 38. King Hezekiah is gravely ill and cries out to God for mercy. The Lord hears his cries and promises to extend his life. Then, in Isaiah 38:21, Isaiah prescribes a medical treatment:

> Now Isaiah had said, "Let them take a cake of figs and apply it to the boil, that he may recover." (Isaiah 38:21)

The God who calls light out of darkness is the same God who, incarnated centuries later, daubed mud on a blind man's eyes. And here in Hezekiah's time he uses a cake of figs to bring recovery to Hezekiah. So, what healed Hezekiah: God or the fig cake?

The answer is yes. As E. J. Young observes, "God is often pleased to use means in the performance of his works."[13]

Some Christians object to this understanding of medicine. They hold that God's activity is distinct from nature, including medicine. Turning to medical help, in their view, is a sign of weak faith in God's ability to heal. 2 Chronicles 16:12 seems to suggest this kind of opposition. King Asa was a good king of Judah who turned evil toward the end of his life. As a result, he contracted an (unspecified) foot disease as an act of God's judgment.

> In the thirty-ninth year of his reign Asa was diseased in his feet, and his disease became severe. Yet even in his disease he did not seek the LORD, but sought help from physicians. (2 Chronicles 16:12)

Rather than seek mercy from the Lord, Asa went to the physicians. Second Chronicles presents this as rebellion.

What was Asa's sin here? At first glance, it might seem as if he sinned by seeking out a physician. (Mark 5:25-26 would, on this read, take a similarly dim view of first-century doctors, for they took 12 years and all of a woman's money and yet failed to heal her.) But Scripture has to be allowed to interpret Scripture in this case. Other minor medical interventions do occur in scriptural stories without apparent condemnation.

How can we harmonize the teaching of 2 Chronicles 16:12 with the testimony of the rest of Scripture, which tells us that God is generally pleased to use human means to do things he could do directly for us? (Indeed, God could deposit money in Christians' bank accounts through computer glitches, but he usually instead gives us vocations and the strength and opportunity to fulfill them.)

We harmonize this passage by focusing on Asa's motive: he did not seek the Lord; he sought the doctors. One way to say this is that he set in contra-distinction what should have been set in conjunction. In other words, he trusted in doctors to the *exclusion* of trusting in God. What he ought to have done was trust that God would work *through* the doctors. It's entirely appropriate for Christians today to do just that—to seek the Lord's hand *through* physicians. Asa's sin was one of attitude and motive rather than of mere action. Seeing treatment from a doctor does not exhibit a lack of faith—as long as you recognize that the Lord is ultimately the one who heals you. Medicine does not function independently from the Lord of all the earth.

In fact, all science, including medical science, arises from a set of presuppositions about the world that are consistent with Scripture. The Creator set up the universe to operate by a set of principles. These can be studied, and to some degree understood and manipulated, because they follow the unchanging laws of one Lawgiver. By contrast, if you believe that a particular sickness is caused by some minor god, such as the Spirit of Bile, there's no telling what treatment might work. Bile spirits are capricious, demanding an herbal root today and a bird-feather poultice tomorrow, so how do you know what to do? But if God's world obeys divinely given natural laws, we can expect that the thermometer readings from under our tongues will display consistent patterns, and that our bodies will respond in basically the same way to Tylenol today as they did yesterday.

God can work his divine purposes through everyday means—he can and does heal through the ordinary means of medicine. Divine healing does not have to be something fantastic and other-worldly. Sometimes it is as simple as cleaning a wound, yet still God is at work in bringing relief. Although ancient medicine was fairly basic, the Bible commends it as a display of God's mercy to the world.

Medicine in the New Testament

One of the leading features of the ministry of Jesus was, of course, his healing. One of the ways he demonstrated the character of the kingdom of God was by making the sick healthy. He gave to his apostles (and, apparently, to some other early Christians) the capacity to heal miraculously. But even within the pages and the time period of the New Testament, God blesses ordinary means of healing as well.

The Good Samaritan

These ordinary means figure prominently in the one parable Jesus told to explain what love for neighbor looks like: the Good Samaritan. This extraordinary neighbor brings God's mercy to a suffering stranger; he spares no expense, providing both medical care and accommodations.

He went to him and bound up his wounds,
pouring on oil and wine. Then he set him on his
own animal and brought him to an inn and took
care of him. (Luke 10:34)

If you were to pour olive oil and cooking wine
from your groceries onto the wounds of a stranger
who lay on the side of the road after a car accident,
he might not appreciate the gesture. But, in fact,
the Good Samaritan was following best practices
for first-century EMTs. Biblical scholar William
Hendriksen observes that the alcohol in wine
would serve both as antiseptic and disinfectant; the
oil would serve as a salve.[14] In the New Testament,
administering medicine is an act of mercy and love.

A Little Wine for Timothy's Stomach

The Apostle Paul's words of wisdom to his protégé
Timothy include this compassionate line:

No longer drink only water, but use a little wine
for the sake of your stomach and your frequent
ailments. (1 Timothy 5:23)

This comment can seem out of place in a
paragraph full of practical wisdom for leading the
church. But what Paul is doing here, under the inspi-
ration of the Holy Spirit, is the same thing friends

do all the time. He's offering a little advice. Judging by the first phrase, "No longer drink only water," Timothy seems to have been abstaining from wine. Paul perceived that this was having a negative impact on his health; Timothy suffered "frequent ailments" because he was cutting himself off from one of God's means of bodily healing.

Why was Timothy abstaining from wine? We can't know with certainty, because the Bible doesn't tell us. Maybe he was honoring an ancestor the way the Rechabites of Jeremiah 35 did. Maybe he was trying to *help* his health. Or maybe he was distancing himself from drunkards. It doesn't matter for our purposes. What matters is what we do know from this verse: living according to the divinely instituted laws of nature—in this case, drinking a little wine for a medicinal purpose—can be a good and spiritual thing to do.

If: Marijuana as Medicine?

In Meredith Wilson's cleverly satirical *The Music Man*, Professor Harold Hill sings, "First it's a little medicinal wine from a teaspoon, then beer from a bottle!" Essentially, he's making fun of people who take on a sanctimonious attitude when warning others about slippery slopes. The truth is, though, that some slippery slopes are real. The innocent, honorable, medicinal use of certain substances can indeed become a gateway into abuse. Harold Hill's joke is not nearly as funny in an age of rampant prescription drug abuse. If one teaspoon of wine is okay (or one Vicodin or Oxycontin), why not two or three?

So this chapter hinges on a big *if*.

If marijuana can have medicinal properties, or can be used to create medicines, the side effects of which fall into the normal range accepted among other drugs, then the fact that it's commonly used to get high doesn't in itself justify keeping it from (for example) epileptic 8-year-olds. This big *if* can be established, however, only by those gifted and trained to do so, using the empirical tools made available by medical science. The purpose of this chapter is merely to establish the biblical parameters surrounding the medical-scientific question.

Abuse of alcohol certainly began long before Paul's day. And yet Paul was still open to medicinal use of this potentially dangerous substance. (This is true whatever the alcohol levels of wine may have been at that time.)

Side effects and the possibility of unintended consequences must be kept in mind, of course. Widespread acceptance of marijuana as medicine could potentially be the wedge our freedom-worshiping Western world uses to make recreational restrictions look ridiculous. In fact, proponents of recreational pot have apparently worked on just this strategy.[15] In all things, however, the Bible calls for prudence and wisdom within the parameters it establishes. Thus, the fact that "something could go wrong" should not be sufficient reason for Christians to want to slam the door on even the possibility of marijuana as medicine.

In the end, legalization of any drug for prescription use is always a matter of weighing potential benefits against potential risks. Some U.S. states *have* legalized medicinal use of marijuana, believing that the science validates such a position. Some doctors in these states then choose to prescribe medicinal marijuana liberally, presumably (apart from a possible profit motive) because they believe current law is too restrictive. True over-prescription, of course, simply results in recreational use by another name, and represents a violation of the biblical commands to obey the governing authorities. It is worth noting, however, that as of this writing, even states that permit recreational use still place limits on that use.

Using Good Gifts with Wisdom

Christian ethics involves a regenerated person applying God's norms to his or her situation.[16] This book focuses on God's norms within Scripture. But God has placed other norms in nature, which are consistent with Scripture, and which we must identify and observe. Those latter norms, relating to natural laws, raise questions which must be answered by any regenerated person evaluating any use of marijuana. Following are some of the more obvious questions.

- What are the overall risks of medicinal marijuana usage?
- Is it a gateway or slippery-slope drug?
- Are there particular side-effects that may apply to the use of marijuana or its derivatives by young children?
- If medical marijuana use is permitted, will improper recreational use increase?
- Is marijuana the most effective treatment or palliation for a particular disease, condition, or patient, or are other more effective ones available?
- How would medicinal marijuana be administered to particular patients facing particular circumstances?
- How should it be controlled?

These are good and important questions, but they are not explicitly biblical questions. We cannot look to a particular chapter and verse to provide guidance. Instead, the answers to such questions come as we study God's created world and apply godly wisdom to questions of public policy. Medical research is necessary to give us a better understanding of the medicinal value of marijuana, if any. Understanding the Bible is necessary to help us interpret and apply that research in a wise and God-honoring way. There is some room for Christians to disagree on the answers to some questions.

Remember our hypothetical discussion about a young Christian mother with an epileptic child who was posing unexpected and difficult questions on Facebook? This book could not explicitly answer her questions. But it could give her something of broader value—the theological framework she needs to bring to the discussion if she hopes to come out with God-pleasing answers to the many questions she is likely to face in the course of her child's care.

God loves the suffering child. While the overall question of suffering in the Christian life is one that has itself taken up many books, the orthodox Christian position on the matter is clear: God's decision to allow the child's seizures is a good one. As Tim Keller has pointed out, if God is big enough to be blamed for the epileptic kids in the world, he has to be big enough to have reasons for that suffering that we can't know.[17]

What we can know is God's divine love. Our God is the Great Physician. He heals broken and hurting people, physically and spiritually. And in the death and resurrection of Christ, God has once and for all defeated death and suffering. We look forward to the day when Jesus will return in glory and destroy all suffering. On that day, medicine will no longer even be necessary because disease and illness will be a distant memory. But until that day comes, we recognize God's acts of mercy through medicine and embrace his gifts with gratitude.

Takeaways for Chapter 3

1. Sometimes God heals through miracles. Other times, he does it through ordinary means. It's God who heals in both cases.
2. The Bible records God using substances, such as alcohol or oils, as a way of healing people. This is (part of) ancient medicine.
3. The Bible doesn't clearly forbid medical uses of marijuana. Competent medical-scientific research is needed to determine whether or not marijuana and its compounds produce beneficial drugs.

Four
MARIJUANA AND ALCOHOL

This is really the hot-button chapter, isn't it? It's probably safe to say that every Christian who favors recreational marijuana use will base his or her argument in large part on what the Bible says about drinking alcohol. In fact, maybe you yourself jumped ahead to this chapter, imagining it's the only one that really matters.

It isn't. The Bible is an integrated whole. So before you ever get to the question of whether marijuana is sufficiently "like" alcohol that it's OK for Christians to use it recreationally, you need the other chapters in this book. You need chapter one as a conceptual foundation, and chapter two as a reality check, while chapter three will give you some tools for thinking biblically about how we use foreign substances to help when someone is hurting. So, please go back and read those chapters if you haven't yet.

The author of this book, who composed the

initial argument, drinks alcohol in moderation. The coauthor, who has tried to make that argument stick with illustrations and an occasional dash of humor (for which he takes sole blame), is a teetotaler who has never taken a sip of alcohol (except once by accident on a mission trip in South America—it looked like fruit juice!). The author drinks occasionally, and does so to the glory of God out of a humble desire to receive God's good gifts in creation. The coauthor, out of a desire to honor his parents and heritage, to be "led not into temptation," and to minister to the down-and-out, plans to save his enjoyment of alcohol for the new earth—when Jesus said he will drink it "new with you in my Father's kingdom" (Matthew 26:29).

But we two brothers in Christ are united in believing that the Bible is our authority, that the Bible's teaching is sufficient for guiding our moral lives, and that the principles discernible behind biblical commands apply beyond the direct statements of Scripture. Otherwise, any sin invented since the first century would be fair game!

Given that all created things are fundamentally good (though not, as we've said, necessarily good for putting in your mouth), and that Paul calls it a "doctrine of devils" to forbid certain things God created good, it is appropriate for us to ask whether marijuana can be used recreationally for the glory of

God. So this chapter (and the book itself) exists for three reasons.

1. Christians have long had a relatively settled position, theologically, on the recreational use of alcohol. Even many personal teetotalers allow that in certain circumstances other believers have the liberty to drink within certain limits.

2. Historically, Christians have also had quite a settled position on marijuana use: almost universally forbidden. Yet this position has been primarily a matter of Christian tradition, rather than theology. And as a practical matter, that's been sufficient, because until recently every law in the land (at least, as written on the books) upheld the overwhelming Christian consensus on this issue.

3. Now that laws are increasingly moving toward the decriminalization of recreational marijuana use (following rapid shifts in cultural acceptance), our knee-jerk opposition is showing itself to be inadequate. We desperately need a clarification of whether Christians should be opposed to recreational marijuana use, and if so, the *biblical* basis for that opposition.

For Christians who are considering whether marijuana *ought* to achieve some of the social and legal legitimacy of alcohol, the commonalities between the two substances give us an opportunity: examining what the Bible says about alcohol is a constructive way forward. Alcohol was without a doubt the drug of choice in biblical times and carries its own mood-altering effects, so it is the best biblical analogy for modern-day marijuana use.[18]

Alcohol in the Old Testament

The general teaching of the Old Testament is that alcohol is *a good thing that is dangerously subject to abuse*. Thus, like many other good things in civil society (automobiles, electrical codes, lending law, etc.), it is nevertheless to be treated with wisdom and moderation, and in accordance with applicable laws and regulations. Some will choose to abstain completely, and that's fine, while others should seriously consider abstaining (see Proverbs 31:4–5).

The most common alcoholic drink of the ancient world was wine, and many of the scriptural statements about alcohol reference wine specifically. Psalm 104:14-15 is perhaps the most famous among them. It praises God directly for several gifts, including alcohol:

> You cause the grass to grow for the livestock
> and plants for man to cultivate,
> that he may bring forth food from the earth

and wine to gladden the heart of man,
oil to make his face shine
and bread to strengthen man's heart.

The same God who gives bread and oil for
strength and health gives wine — and it's instructive
that wine's stated purpose is to "gladden the heart
of man." Wine is a divine gift for bringing humans
joy. Somewhere between the mind-altering buzz of
drunkenness and the effect of non-alcoholic grape
juice is something God calls "gladdening the heart."

Alcohol and the drink offering. This joy and
gladness is why God establishes the drink offering
as part of the sacrificial system (see Exodus 29:38-46;
Numbers 15:7; 1 Chronicles 29:20-22). The drink
offering was a way for God's people to eat and drink
with God. It was supposed to be a place of intimate
relationship and joy. Sin had removed man's fellowship with God but, through the sacrificial system,
God (partially) restored it. The system of offerings —
including one in which people literally poured
alcohol onto an altar — looked forward to the day
when God would fully restore his broken relationship with them through the death and resurrection
of Jesus.

Alcohol and the tithe. The specific instructions
God gives for the tithe in Deuteronomy 14:22–29
illustrate the same idea: that the good gifts of God,

including alcohol, are meant to aid joyful fellowship with God. The passage acknowledges that for some ancient Jews, the place that God chose for them to bring their tithe was too far away for them to travel with crops. But God loved them and still desired to have this personal moment with his people, so he made provisions for these individuals. They could sell their tithed crops and use the money to buy an offering instead:

> Then you shall turn it into money and bind up the money in your hand and go to the place that the LORD your God chooses and spend the money for whatever you desire—oxen or sheep or wine or strong drink, whatever your appetite craves. And you shall eat there before the LORD your God and rejoice, you and your household. (Deuteronomy 14:25-26)

Not only is God inviting his people to eat with him, he is also inviting them to share a drink with him. They should buy whatever they desire and bring it to the divine table. But the important point is that they should come and be with their God. God desires the kind of fellowship with his people that sitting at a table together uniquely provides, and alcohol has an appropriate place in their fellowship.

But the Old Testament carries warnings about

wine and other alcoholic beverages as well. Our sinful hearts quickly twist God's good gifts; alcohol is not exempt from the effects of human rebellion. The misuse of alcohol is shown over and over in the Old Testament to bring tragedy and destruction.

Noah

The Bible's first mention of alcohol is one such moment. After God judicially kills every living being on earth for their wickedness — except the inhabitants of one boat — the narrative shows that wickedness made it onto the boat through the humans aboard. In Genesis 9, Noah plants a vineyard and gets drunk, an action which ends up embarrassing him and causing trouble in the family. The very first recorded sin after the flood, the sin that shows that the human slate cannot be wiped clean even by the most extraordinary means, is drunkenness. Noah, the brave servant who obeyed God in the face of divine judgment, is reduced to a comedic spectacle because he drank excessively.

Lot

The dangers of alcohol go far beyond making us look like fools. The Old Testament also recognizes that drunkenness can lead people to take advantage of others. Sometimes predators prey on drunk people, recognizing that they are unable to think clearly, make wise decisions, or sometimes even defend themselves. Moreover, people will do things when they are drunk that they would not do otherwise— and some get drunk for that very reason—but the results are just as harmful.

This is what happened in Genesis 19:30-38. Lot had taken his family to live in the hills, safe from the people of Zoar who might wish them harm. This left Lot's daughters without ready access to men, so there was no one to marry or with whom start a family. So the daughters came up with a deeply disturbing plan. They decided to get their father drunk and have children by him. Their reasoning was that Lot wouldn't know what he was doing if he was drunk. In fact, verse 33 says that Lot was so drunk he didn't even notice when his daughters lay down or when they arose. Lot was so drunk that he was oblivious to what was happening. And their unspeakable plan worked. Both of these women became pregnant by their father.

Now, the daughters clearly carry the greatest burden of guilt here. They're the ones who planned to commit incest with their father and got him drunk to do it. They're the predators in this story. But had Lot remained sober, it's very unlikely that their plan would have worked. If he hadn't been passed out from alcohol, then he could have noticed his daughters entering his bed. Wisdom and moderation offered to protect his wits, but his foolish behavior—

his obvious willingness to drink to excess—left him vulnerable instead.

The two children born by these incestuous acts became the fathers of the Moabites and Ammonites, two of Israel's great enemies. Lot's carelessness not only brought great shame on him, it would also hurt God's people far into the future.

Good narratives don't tend to spell out their moral lessons explicitly. And good readers don't need a line at the end of Lot's story that says, "Beware: drunkenness leads to loss of self-control!" The story of Lot in Genesis says it all: if you want to avoid unsound moral decisions, don't get drunk.

Proverbs

As a collection of wise sayings, a book written from father (and mother, Proverbs 31:1) to children, Proverbs naturally has a great deal to say about drunkenness. For example, Proverbs 23:20-21 puts into poetry a lesson about overindulgence, especially with respect to alcohol, that is illustrated in every major city every day:

> Be not among drunkards
> or among gluttonous eaters of meat,
> for the drunkard and the glutton will come to poverty,
> and slumber will clothe them with rags.

It's not someone who eats meat that is at risk of poverty. It's a glutton who eats *too much* meat. Likewise, it's not the person who drinks any alcohol who is the drunkard. It's the person who drinks *too much* alcohol. This person is at risk of poverty.

God called mankind to fill, subdue, and have dominion over the earth. God gave Adam, and by extension all of us, a job. Work is part of humanity's very design. This includes our regular occupations as employees, employers, freelancers, parents, students, etc. Indeed, adults who for whatever reason cannot work are often left in despair, feeling less than human. But God's design for human work also goes beyond that. Work in the Bible is more than just our day jobs. We are made to bring fruitfulness into the world in everything we do. This includes our work as parents — even as children and siblings. It includes our social time. In these shared moments, we are doing the work of encouraging and building up others. Even in our rest and relaxation, we reflect upon the fruitfulness that God has brought into the world through work, and we rest for the work to come.

Gluttony and drunkenness both impair our ability to work for the glory of God and the good of others. How productive are you after stuffing yourself on Thanksgiving? The only people working after that are the dishwashers and the football players, hired to entertain all us couch potatoes. Excessive eating seriously compromises our ability to be fruitful.

So it is with alcohol. One who consumes too much alcohol and becomes drunk is unable to do any meaningful work. Both thinking and speech are slurred. Motor skills become less precise. Drunkenness, like gluttony, actually deprives us of our ability to fulfill our created design. And God says don't do it.

Total Abstinence and the Old Testament

The technology of distillation has advanced considerably since ancient times. There is no simple one-to-one correspondence between the "wine" of Noah's or Jesus' day and the sometimes fortified wines of today. The alcohol content in some beverages today is so high that they seem designed for the very purpose of getting people drunk quickly.

Combine this with the horrendous effects of alcohol on Western society—the eroded livers, the fatherless children, the physical and sexual violence, the fatal car accidents—and many Christians, understandably, choose not to drink at all. There are also Bible passages which call on us to consider the effects of our actions on weaker brothers (Romans 14:20), and whether or not something has power over us (1 Corinthians 6:12).

Yet it is difficult, in light of the positive things

the Bible says about alcohol, to conclude *no one* should drink. Yes, the Bible seems to suggest that wine in Bible times was diluted with water (history and archaeology bear this out), but even if our knowledge of those cultural practices was clear and unambiguous, it would still be difficult to argue biblically against all consumption of beverage alcohol.[19]

Christians who hold strongly to complete abstinence for all believers often cite Proverbs 23:30-31 as teaching that all alcohol is sinful:

> Those who tarry long over wine;
> those who go to try mixed wine.
> Do not look at wine when it is red,
> when it sparkles in the cup
> and goes down smoothly.

How is it possible, however, to read this as a condemnation of all beverage alcohol given the positive passages we've referenced? Viewed in context, Proverbs 23:30–31 is focused on drunkenness, not on all beverage use of alcohol. The paragraph identifies some perils of drinking alcohol, including things like strange visions, perverse speech and desires, (23:33) and insensitivity to the consequences of one's binging (23:34-35). Clearly, these are not descriptions of what happens after one glass of wine.

On the one hand, we should never take the teeth

out of this passage: some Christians do violate it, and can suffer serious consequences as a result. On the other, alcohol in the Old Testament is good for the way it cheers people. It is good for the kind of close relationships it can foster—as seen by its place in the sacrificial system. But alcohol is subject to abuse and misuse. Wrong use brings a drunkenness which robs us of clear thinking and our capacity for God-given fruitfulness.

So the Bible sees alcohol for the two-edged sword that it is. If used in moderation, it is a gift. If used in excess, it is a curse.

Alcohol in the New Testament

The biblical perspective on alcohol does not change when moving from Old Testament to New.

The Wedding at Cana

For Jesus' very first miracle, he provided alcohol for guests to drink at a wedding. Weddings then featured wine, as many do now, and when the wedding party at Cana ran out, Jesus' mother Mary immediately turns to him in hopes that he can do something. Jesus responds by turning six containers of water into wine, resulting in somewhere between 120 and 180 gallons of wine. It's worth noting that, for many of the guests, this clearly would not have been their first drink at that wedding, either (John 2:9-10).

Any trained PR person would likely have advised Jesus that raising the dead or healing the sick might have been a better way to begin the miraculous aspect of his ministry. Planting a money tree would probably have been a big hit, too. So, why this particular miracle?

The Bible doesn't tell us. All we get is the general comment that everything recorded about Jesus' ministry was "written so that you may believe that Jesus is the Christ, the Son of God" (John 20:31). How does the turning of water into wine produce faith in Jesus? Many careful Bible students have noted that Jesus' miracles show what the kingdom of God will be like when it fully comes. This miracle demonstrates that Christ has power over this cursed world to make it new again.

It also shows that Christ is no religious hermit or monk, uninterested in the kinds of things that mark real life—like weddings and wine. Indeed, the New Testament says that Christ in the new earth will restore everything to the way it ought to be. Grapes ought to be plentiful, producing much wine. And wine ought to be good, gladdening the heart of man.

Jesus not only made wine, he also drank wine. The Pharisees even called Jesus a glutton and a drunkard. They accused the creator of the good gifts of food and alcohol of abusing those gifts (largely because he spent time pursuing the souls of those who did abuse them). But because Jesus is without sin, he was free to enjoy his own gifts to humanity without misusing them—and in so doing to bear witness to a better way. Jesus could eat without gluttony and drink without drunkenness.

The Last Supper

So, the first thing Jesus did in his public ministry was provide wine to guests at a wedding feast. And the last thing he did in his public ministry was provide bread and wine to friends at a Passover meal. Like the offerings prescribed in Deuteronomy, God (in this case, God the Son) wanted to share food and drink in close relationship with people.

When Jesus handed the "fruit of the vine" to the twelve disciples, he handed them a symbol of the very thing that made his fellowship with them possible. Unholy people can sit down with a holy God only through the blood of Christ, symbolized by the Passover wine. When we today drink the wine (or juice) of the Lord's Supper, we do it in remembrance of the blood sacrifice that makes it possible for us, too, to fellowship with God himself.

Pauline Epistles

Paul's letters also provide instruction on the use of alcohol. In 1 Corinthians 6:12, Paul makes what may at first appear to be a dangerously libertarian statement: "All things are lawful for me." But he immediately makes two qualifications, both of which are relevant to alcohol. "All things are lawful for me…"

1. "but not all things are helpful."
2. "but I will not be dominated by anything."

If alcohol is lawful, it is certainly not always helpful. If it is lawful, it certainly has the power to dominate. That's what we call drunkenness: domination by alcohol. And Paul is deeply concerned about drunkenness. In Galatians 5:19-21, he lists drunkards among the unrepentant sinners who will not inherit the kingdom of God.

In two other Pauline lists — qualifications for church elders — not being a drunkard shows up both times (1 Timothy 3:3; Titus 1:7). If drunkenness leads to foolish and harmful decisions, then those who are making decisions on behalf of God's people must remain sober. Drunkenness lowers our inhibitions and makes it more likely that we will give in to certain temptations to sin. Elders are people too; they face the same temptations every Christian does. It is important for elders to model faithful, holy living.

But these qualifications aren't just relevant to church leaders. They're instructive for all Christians. The Bible's qualifications for elders are overwhelmingly about character rather than skill, because the portrait is that of a mature and faithful Christian. These are the men who should lead God's church. If the image is of maturity in faith, then these characteristics are surely instructive for all Christians.

Alcohol and Marijuana

Now let's draw connections between alcohol and marijuana.

The two are, admittedly, not precisely parallel. Marijuana is typically smoked or eaten, and alcohol is drunk. The effects of alcohol are well known throughout the Western world, those of marijuana less so. However, both substances affect the mind, and this is key. Doug Wilson observes that it is noteworthy that:

> The only thing that pot does for you — get you buzzed — is the one use prohibited concerning alcohol. When Paul tells us not to be drunk with wine, he did not mean that getting drunk with beer or scotch was acceptable. The problem is not the wine, but rather the loss of self-control. And because such mental impairment is the whole *point* of smoking pot, recreational marijuana use is a serious sin, from the very first toke on down. No one smokes pot because it pairs nicely with the fish.[20]

In other words, since lack of self control appears to be the principle behind the Bible's condemnation of drunkenness, the comparison between marijuana and alcohol is valid, even if it is not exact.

It is sinful to get high for the same reasons it is to get drunk. Being high lowers inhibitions, clouds decision making, and deprives people of fruitfulness in their work. Alcohol and marijuana share this danger. So we can conclude that the Bible forbids getting high just as it condemns drunkenness. Smoking marijuana recreationally in order to get high is sinful.

Marijuana in Moderation?

But the Bible allows Christians to drink alcohol in moderation so long as they do not get drunk. Is this option open for marijuana? Can Christians smoke pot as long as they do not get high?

This book has consistently backed away from making authoritative observations about the effects of marijuana, medical or otherwise. Once again, finding out the truth about these effects would require empirical study that goes beyond the scope of this narrowly focused book.

In addition, not all claimants to the title of "empirical" are created equal. On such a hotly debated topic as pot, the danger is high that whoever funds a given study (whether the libertarian or the prohibitionist) will get the answer he or she pays for.

However, what follows are a few suggestions based on what appear to be reliable sources:

1. **It takes very little marijuana to get high.** How much exactly depends on a person's individual tolerance and the potency of the drug itself (various strains of marijuana have different levels of potency). The National Highway Traffic Safety Administration in the United States considered this question of potency when considering the risks of marijuana for drivers. Their report says, "1-3 hits of high potency *sinsemilla* is typically enough to produce the desired effects."[21] A "hit" is defined *a single intake of smoke*. So whereas people drink *without* getting drunk every day around the world, and there is significant space between a sip and an alcohol buzz (depending on the drink), the NHTSA's point is that it is very unlikely that a person will smoke marijuana without getting high.[22] If this is true, then the recreational use of marijuana is sinful because of the Bible's teaching on intoxication.

2. **Smoking is a dangerous way to ingest any substance, even a beneficial one.** Whether the active ingredient delivered by the smoke is nicotine from tobacco or THC from marijuana, similar substances come along for the ride into the lungs.[23]

3. **Governments worldwide have banned marijuana.**[24] Are they all just giving in to the tobacco and alcohol lobbies, who are secretly paying politicians to keep marijuana illegal? No, if governments, despite their flaws, are God's ministers to us for our good (Romans 13), perhaps we ought to give them the benefit of the doubt. The law-enforcement arm of government necessarily knows things about marijuana use from up-close experience, things most of us cannot know because our callings don't put us in regular contact with drug abusers.

4. **Anecdotal evidence carries a consistent theme: stoners become dominated by their weed.** Anecdotes do not provide sufficient information for policy-making, but to rely on anecdotal evidence is not in itself invalid. We all do it all the time; not every question can be studied empirically before we have to make a decision. One author (Mark Ward) asked children of the 1960s and 1970s about their views on weed, and they all remembered specific people whose lives went nowhere after they began smoking marijuana regularly. The stories were distinctly reminiscent of Proverbs 23's comments about the drunkard: *They struck me…but I was not hurt; they beat me, but I did not feel it. When shall I awake? I must have another puff.* Now, was marijuana a cause

or an effect—or both—of these people's eventual pitiful condition? Personal experience can't tell us for sure. But it ought not be discounted. Perhaps there are recreational marijuana users who smoke without trying to get high, but this really does not seem to be the case. If the purpose of smoking marijuana recreationally is to get high from it, that is no different than drinking with the intention of getting drunk.

A Thought Experiment

Assume for a moment that you live someplace where there are no laws against recreational marijuana use, enforced or unenforced, by any level of government having authority over you (in the United States, as of this writing, there is no such place). Assume also that no one who plays a key role in your life (parents, a spouse, pastors, accountability partners, mentors) would disapprove of you using pot recreationally. Finally, for the sake of argument, assume your conscience is clear: you believe you can smoke or ingest marijuana with no harm, temporary or permanent, to your health or mental capacity.

Even if all those assumptions were to hold, you would still have to face the intoxication question honestly. The point of recreational marijuana use is not to enhance the moment, as is the case with the biblical use of alcohol. The point is to escape from or radically alter the experience of the moment, to chemically force your body and mind into an altered state of a kind that can only qualify as intoxication — a place the Bible plainly tells us not to go.

* * *

You are now almost at the end of *Can I Smoke Pot? – Marijuana in Light of Scripture.* The question posed by the title has ultimately been answered in the negative, because of our plumbline named in the subtitle. At this point then, this book is essentially over…but not completely.

You've probably seen at least one movie that has what filmmakers call a tag or coda. That's when the film ends, the unexpectedly odd music is playing, the credits are endlessly rolling, and most people have already turned off the screen or left the theatre. All of a sudden, however, the screen springs to life. There are the familiar characters…in a new scene…and it actually turns out to be important!

That's how you can think about the closing section of this book. Don't miss it.

Takeaways for Chapter 4
1. Alcohol is a gift that God gives to the world to be used in moderation and in keeping with one's conscience.

2. Drunkenness is the abuse of that gift. Such abuse robs us of our fruitfulness and our self-control. The Bible teaches that Christians may drink alcohol, but it adamantly condemns the sin of drunkenness.

3. Getting high is sinful for the same reasons getting drunk with alcohol is sinful: at minimum, one loses control over one's actions.

Marijuana and You
A CLOSING WORD

Presumably, you picked up this book because you would like to know if Scripture provides any conceivable support for the recreational use of marijuana. If that's your question, then you probably come from one of two perspectives:

1. You would like to use marijuana recreationally with a clear conscience, just as millions of Christians drink alcohol in moderation with full assurance that this does not displease God.
2. You do not have that desire, but you want to be prepared for conversations with people who do.

Once again (because we can't be too clear on these things), what have we seen in this book?

Creation. Like everything else God formed at creation, marijuana is good—although that's not the same as saying it's good for all possible uses. Part of our dominion mandate is to figure out the right and wrong ways to use God's good gifts to further his goals for the world. Sometimes Scripture gives us clear guidance in a given area, but other times we have to extrapolate as best we can from the Bible and from creation. What can the Bible and experience tell us about what marijuana may be good for and not good for?

Government. One of God's good creations is civil government; its authority structures come straight from God (Romans 13:1 ff.). Christians are called to bring a general attitude of submission to even imperfect governments and flawed authorities (and none of them are perfect or flawless). This means that if any applicable authority forbids your recreational marijuana use, that alone is enough reason for you to abstain.

Medicine. When it comes to a vast range of things we may ingest, inhale, absorb, or inject—whether it's food, oxygen, medicine, vitamins, alcohol, or even water—the difference between "good for you" and "bad for you" is generally a matter of factors such as dosage, concentration, frequency, and means of administration. This book has concluded that the Bible does not rule out the possibility that there are beneficial medical uses for the chemical compounds in marijuana.

Alcohol. Many people use alcohol and

marijuana (separately or together) for essentially the same purpose—to achieve a state of intoxication. But drunkenness is precisely the use of alcohol that Scripture forbids. And in the case of marijuana, as a practical matter, intoxication (getting high) seems to be the whole point; it is the goal, the purpose, and the nearly inevitable result of putting THC into one's bloodstream via smoking or ingesting. The thing we are *forbidden* by Scripture to do with alcohol appears to be just about the only thing we can *possibly* do with marijuana recreationally.

We, the authors, are well aware that a book on this subject could be much longer, much more detailed, much more thorough, and far more philosophically nuanced. But for one thing, most people wouldn't read that book. More importantly, we're confident that if the authors of any such book were determined to allow Scripture to be their ultimate guide, they would still come to the same ultimate conclusion.

In the light of Scripture, Christians are not at liberty to consume marijuana recreationally.

This is not a debatable application of an obscure New Testament Greek verb. If nothing else, it is a good and necessary consequence of the command not to get drunk. As such, it bears the authority of God. Are Christians free to explore medical uses of the compounds in marijuana? Yes, within established medical-scientific bounds. Can Christians smoke or otherwise ingest pot in any way that reflects the means or motivations for which it is popularly consumed? No.

Seriously? But I Still Want to Get High...

If that's your position, and you claim to be a Christian who believes the Bible to be the true, inspired, authoritative, and unchanging Word of God, then please let us close with this appeal to you.

Some who smoke pot consider it a matter of relaxing or destressing. Taking some time, maybe at the end of the day, to escape from everything. Unplug. Unwind. Chill. That's not intoxication, right? That's just kicking back. Why would God mind?

If you've come to that point...if you're actually splitting hairs about what is intoxication and what isn't, or appealing to uncertainties in the science, or ignoring the main points of the government chapter pertaining not just to laws but to the opinions of others in your life, please look very closely at your motivations.

Where does this drive to justify getting high come from? What are you really craving, and why are you pushing this point so hard? Is it peer pressure? Is it an escapism that denies some area of sin or brokenness in your life? Are you effectively seeking a kind of palliative care (addressed in the Medicine chapter) to soothe some emotional or spiritual pain in your life? A pain that God will gladly soothe if you only draw near to him through his Word and prayer?

These are the real questions behind all your objections and would-be justifications. These are the issues you should be probing deeply and honestly. These are the matters you should be bringing before God, trusting that even in those struggles, he is doing you good (Romans 8:28).

God is better than drunkenness. He is better than getting high. And he is opposed to both those things because they are false and harmful escapes—pitiful, idolatrous substitutes for the experience of his presence and favor. If you are a Christian, the experience of God's unending love and mercy can be richly and abundantly yours if you reach out to him.

Seek the better, higher, more noble, more beautiful thing. Seek God.

About the Authors

Tom Breeden received an M.Div. from Reformed Theological Seminary in Washington, D.C. and is currently licensed by the Blue Ridge Presbytery of the Presbyterian Church in America (PCA). He currently serves as the Pastoral Intern at Grace Community Church in Charlottesville, VA.

Mark L. Ward, Jr. received his PhD from Bob Jones University in 2012; he now serves the church as a Logos Pro at Faithlife, writing weekly articles on Bible study at the Logos Talk Blog. He is the author of multiple high school Bible textbooks, including *The Story of the Old Testament* and *Biblical Worldview: Creation, Fall, Redemption*.

Appendix
HOW TO USE THE BIBLE TO ANSWER YOUR QUESTIONS

by Peter Krol, Author of *Knowable Word: Helping Ordinary People Learn to Study the Bible*

"If you can't use the Bible to answer your questions, you don't really understand it."

Without apology, Tom Breeden and Mark Ward stake everything on the premise that the Bible can and should answer our questions, and that reasonable, postmodern people must be competent in putting the Bible to this use. We, the readers, have now heard the authors' straightforward question: Can Christians smoke pot? We've considered the authors' reasoning concerning creation, government, medicine, and alcohol. And we've received a forthright answer: No. But now we must return to that unapologetic opening premise to see if it withstands scrutiny. Is it a deceptively poisonous form of spiritual bravado, or can we actually bet our lives on it?

In short: Can we trust these fallible and opinionated contemporaries of ours to use a mysterious and ancient text to make smart decisions? And can we follow in their train? If so, how?

Many People Use the Bible to Answer Their Questions

But before getting to the how, let's first address a concern some may have. Many people use the Bible for help with their questions, and they often come up with radically different answers from one another. Who are we to say one person's interpretation is right and another's is wrong? Breeden and Ward's conclusion might work fine for them; but who can say it's the best conclusion for everyone?

This same objection could take another form: Many people in history have used the Bible to oppress and harm weaker people. How can we be sure Breeden and Ward aren't doing the same by trying to deny marijuana to people who would simply enjoy it?

That right and wrong exist (including right and

wrong answers) is indisputable—how else could it be *wrong* to assert there is right and wrong? So the logic and techniques we use to figure out the difference between the two genuinely matter. Still, that doesn't change the fact that sometimes harmful differences exist among those who claim to trust the Bible.

> For example, you can pick up any tract from the Watchtower Society to find Bible-saturated arguments that Jesus is not God, the Holy Spirit is not a person, God's kingdom was established in 1914, holiday celebrations are sacrilegious, and blood transfusions are immoral. Or, closer to the topic at hand, you can Google biblical defense of marijuana to find many who, using the Bible, reach an opposite conclusion to Breeden and Ward. In fact, as long as you look at just one specific translation, God did, in fact, promise to raise up a "plant of renown" for his people (Ezekiel 34:29, AV).[25]

If different people use the same Bible to reach different conclusions, some might question the act of reaching conclusions—as though the different conclusions prove we can't reach true conclusions. But such a conclusion only compounds the problem. In fact, I don't recommend ever *concluding* that we can't reach true conclusions (and wouldn't it be ironic if we did).

A better response to the variety of conclusions is to *question the way people use the Bible to reach their conclusions*. Therefore, we need not be intimidated by the fact that differences exist among Bible interpreters. These differences don't mean we can't draw accurate conclusions from the Bible. These differences simply mean we must pay careful attention to *how those different people use the Bible*. In other words, the variety of conclusions should cause us to scrutinize the methodology that led to those conclusions. Perhaps the solution to our concern lies there.

A Simple and Reasonable Method

In order to use the Bible to answer our questions, and to do so legitimately, we need a way to move from the ancient text to contemporary ethics. And if Breeden and Ward are correct that the readers of this book, and anyone else for that matter, should be able to make this move, the method must not be complicated. While we need the research of scholars to preserve and deepen knowledge, our fundamental method for Bible use must not require a graduate education or academic pedigree. Nor must it assume a library of knowledge or a specific set of cultural expectations.

If Breeden and Ward are correct—that you don't understand the Bible if you can't use it to answer your questions—there must be a simple method for Bible study that transcends history, geography, generational divides, and cultural norms. This method must not bore scholars, and it must not leave school children behind. It should take moments to learn and a lifetime to perfect. It should work for anyone of any age in any place at any time.

You have such a method already, and you use it all the time. You're using it right now. You follow this method every time you communicate with another person, dead or alive, through written or oral means. Perhaps you do it so instinctively you've never thought of it as a method.

1. Observe—What does it say?
2. Interpret—What does it mean?
3. Apply—How should I respond?

That's it. Your toddler niece does it when she *observes* her mother hand her a bottle, she *interprets* the gesture as an offer of liquid treasure, and she *applies* the event's meaning by seizing the bottle and taking a swig. Someone's great-great-great grandpa did it back in the Old World when he *observed* a customer enter his humble shop, he *interpreted* the arrival as potential business, and he *applied* the situation by smiling, welcoming, and pitching his wares.

Think about reading the news, hearing a lecture, talking on the phone, communicating non-verbally with someone you just met, attending a business meeting, listening to music, watching TV, debating an issue, texting, or going on a date. Every act of meaningful communication between two individuals—even when done across time through a book—can be broken down into three steps: Observe, Interpret, and Apply.

OIA. It's really that simple.

How OIA Helps Us to Use the Bible Well

What would happen if you ignored any of the steps? Imagine you're a homebuilder, and the buyer has communicated his intentions to you through a series of plans. Fail to *observe* the plans, and you'll end up with an "interesting" house not up to code or customer satisfaction. Fail to *interpret* the plans, and you may end up with a geothermally heated yacht, completely missing the designer's intention. Fail to *apply* the plans, and you won't stay in business for long; nobody wants to pay you to go golfing.

Picture how challenging it can be to communicate with someone lacking one or more of the three skills. Those who consistently fail to apply what is communicated to them, we might call lazy or irresponsible. Those unable to interpret the main ideas, we consider aloof or socially awkward. And when someone can't or won't observe the facts, we look for evidence of disability. In each case, we must adjust our expectations and fill in the gaps before communication can take place.

God has communicated to us through his word, the Bible. And communication hits its mark through OIA. So to understand what God has spoken, we must use the OIA method on the Bible. What matters most is not the exact terminology of OIA, but the substance of it. Many people say the same thing with different terminology; COMA, SOAR, CIA, the Swedish Method, and the grammatical-historical method of biblical interpretation are all essentially OIA by different names. So when I say "we must use the OIA method on the Bible," please don't misread me to be saying "anyone who doesn't use the terms *observe*, *interpret*, and *apply* must be misusing the Bible." I'm merely saying we must read the Bible the same way we normally communicate with other people.

So how do normal people do this in their Bible study?

Observe

Great Bible study begins with a few basic

mechanics.[26] Whether you're an untested rookie or a seasoned professional, you can always improve at observing these five categories.

1. Genre. Is this passage poetry or prose? A letter or a narrative? A prophecy, a collection of wisdom, or a song?

2. Words. Count how many times key words are repeated. Notice how various things are described or labeled. Keep track of how the narrator names the characters through the passage, and whether he changes their names or titles along the way.

3. Grammar. Identify the subject, verb, and object of each sentence. What are the main verbs? (This isn't as scary as it sounds; you're just looking for the actors and their actions.) In other words: who does what, and to whom or what is it done?

4. Structure. How does the passage fit together? Break it into paragraphs or stanzas. Notice transitions.

5. Mood. What tone does the author use? Does the passage inspire action, evoke emotion, or challenge assumptions?

Let me illustrate these categories of observation with some examples from the present book:

- **Genre.** In chapter 3, the Palliative Care in Proverbs 31 section, Breeden and Ward take time to observe the genre of a wisdom passage, because that observation affects how they read the text.
- **Words.** In the opening section of chapter 1, the authors observe the repetition of *good* in Genesis 1, and this leads them to assert repeatedly that marijuana is part of God's "good" creation.
- **Grammar.** In chapter 2, the Creation and Government section, they take time to observe some grammar, listing all the actions Adam and Eve were to perform in their exercise of dominion over the earth.
- **Structure.** In chapter 4, in the Proverbs section, the structure (and especially the context) of Proverbs 23 clarifies whether *all* alcohol use is being prohibited, or merely drunkenness.
- **Mood.** In chapter 4, in the Alcohol in the Old Testament section, the mood of Psalm 104 drives a point regarding wine's purpose of gladdening man's heart.

Without careful observation, your study will never find an anchor within the text. Therefore, observation is a critical first step.

OBSERVATION
Genre, words,
grammar, structure, mood

INTERPRETATION
Q&A (what, why,
so what?)

Bible
Times

AUTHOR'S MAIN POINT

Gospel

Now

APPLICATION
Inward & outward
(head, heart, hands)

Interpret

The OIA method can be diagrammed in the shape of a big X. To interpret, we assemble and investigate our many observations until we understand the text's meaning. Since we'll continue observing new things in God's Word until Jesus returns, our observations could be infinite in number. But *interpretations* are not infinite (though our grasp of them may mature over time). Biblical authors had agendas, and we are not authorized to add to those agendas. We investigate the facts of the text until we're able to think the author's thoughts after him. And since biblical authors wrote God's very words, good interpretation trains us to think God's thoughts. It's like when husbands and wives complete each other's sentences, only better.

Three steps will help you conduct a sound and responsible investigation.

Ask questions of your observations. Take your observations and ask lots of questions about them. Tackle those observations from every direction. Be as inquisitive as possible. Get better at asking questions, and you'll get better at interpreting.

Your *questions* should be about your *observations* of the text. Don't ask every question that comes to mind, and don't feel the need to be clever. Your job is not to innovate, but to uncover. If your observation was poor, your interpretation won't be any better. (Note how the disciples didn't observe well, and so jumped to the wrong conclusion in John 21:22–23.)

Answer the questions from the text. Once you've asked your questions, answer them. There's one critical rule: answer questions only if they are answered — explicitly or implicitly — in the text (Proverbs 30:5–6). Don't chase rabbits through the trails of your mind. Don't use minor details to make the text say what you want it to say. Don't build a theology from one unclear verse. Instead, answer only those questions that are either assumed or addressed in the text. Let the rest go.

Determine the author's main point. Your investigation should lead you to the main point of the passage. Sometimes the author's main point is explicit (for example, Hebrews 8:1), but many times it's not. Either way, uncovering the main point should be the goal of interpretation.

The main points of the Bible are the ones worth fighting for because they represent the main things God wants us to understand. We may draw conclusions about secondary or debatable points, but such conclusions must never drown out the Bible's main points in our thinking or teaching (Matthew 23:23–24).

With these three steps and a healthy dose of God's Holy Spirit, you're ready to interpret. Let me illustrate these principles with a few examples from the present book. Of course, the book rests solidly on a major interpretive question: Can Christians smoke pot?

- Chapter 1, under the Creation and Marijuana heading, offers a good example of wrestling through a difficult interpretive question from a particular text: "If the body is bad, then why did God call it good? Adam had flesh, didn't he? And if it's temporary, why does Jesus still have a physical body at this moment?"
- Chapter 2 is filled with interpretive answers: Government is a God-created good. Beings who bear the divine image have inestimable worth. Obedience to human government is an important part of Christian discipleship. And so on. Search for yourself to see whether these answers arise directly from the passages under consideration.
- In Chapter 2, in the section labeled Human Government and the Influence of Sin, the authors use the *main point* of Romans 13 to argue against the rabbit trails of potential objections (e.g., *but governments can make corrupt rules!*).

Sometimes, when we speak about Bible study, we really mean Bible *interpretation*. But let's take note of the fact that good interpretation must arise from careful *observation* and press on to clear and vibrant *application*. Too many "biblical" arguments claim to interpret but fail to observe or apply (for example, consider the Watchtower tracts I mentioned above).

Apply

Christians should be the hardest workers, the most delightful neighbors, and the most trustworthy companions. Why? Not because we need anyone to be impressed with our performance, but because...

- We've been bought with a price and now get to honor God with our bodies (1 Corinthians 6:20).
- We have a new master, and we work for him, not (ultimately) for any human supervisors (Colossians 3:23–24).
- We know what it's like to be forgiven much (Luke 7:47–48).
- Jesus is making all things new (Revelation 21:5), not only in our spiritual lives but also through our relationships, reputation, and work ethic.

Then why do outsiders so often see Christians as lazy, condescending, irritable, and ignorant? On the one hand, lots of people who call themselves Christian may not be, so this doesn't help the overall reputation of actual believers. But even among people of real faith we are, as a general rule, nothing too special—and the Bible says exactly that! God frequently chooses to adopt into his family the powerless and unimpressive so that, as he works through us to change the world, he receives greater glory (1 Corinthians 1:26–31).

So while Jesus is in the business of changing people, he has to start somewhere. He has to start with you and me—and that leaves plenty of room for improvement, doesn't it? Nevertheless, over time, he makes the unlovely lovely. He takes the weak and gives them his strength. He makes the poor rich in him, and the ignorant wise in him. If you follow him, he'll shape you into something useful and guarantee you a part in the greatest drama in the universe.

Therefore, Bible application is the challenging art of producing change. We develop proficiency at this skill by considering three spheres: head, heart, and hands. These spheres represent three aspects of human life where we can both change and be changed. As we will see, Paul suggested these three spheres of application when he taught his protégé Timothy how to use the Bible.

The head represents everything we think and believe. Head application means being a hearer of the Word of God. This sphere involves thinking God's thoughts after him and believing what he says. In this sphere, we meditate on the attributes and nature of God the Father, Son, and Holy Spirit. We identify the lies we believe and replace them with the truth. We remember the gospel, as Paul suggested to Timothy, with our heads: "But as for you, continue in what you have learned and have firmly believed, knowing from whom you learned it and how from childhood you have been acquainted with the sacred writings, which are able to make you wise for salvation through faith in Christ Jesus" (2 Timothy 3:14–15).

The heart represents who we are. Heart application is the first and foundational part of being a doer of the Word. This sphere involves walking in righteousness, desiring the Lord above all, and showing godly wisdom and selfless character. As the seed of the gospel takes deep root, we set aside our old loves and instead begin to love God and others. The gospel, now internalized, shapes our hearts according to the Lord's own righteousness. "All Scripture is breathed out by God and profitable for teaching, for reproof, for correction, and for training in righteousness" (2 Timothy 3:16).

The hands represent everything we do. Hands application is the second part of being a doer of the Word. This sphere involves laying aside our old patterns of selfish behavior, imitating the Lord and his ambassadors, and becoming more effective at building God's Kingdom. Thus, the gospel begins to bear fruit "that the man of God may be complete, equipped for every good work" (2 Timothy 3:17).

God wants to produce change in all three spheres—head, heart, and hands—but many people naturally incline toward only one or two. The trick of application is to address all three areas without imbalance.

When it comes to application in the present book, the authors once again model these Bible-study skills.

- They apply the Scriptures to the *head* by helping us to believe that recreational marijuana use fits well within the Bible's category of drunkenness.
- They apply the Scriptures to the *heart* by avoiding reckless legalism when they open the door to legal exploration of marijuana's medical uses through controlled research. In addition, they push readers toward increased self-control, godward orientation, and selfless submission to the appointed authorities.
- They apply the Scriptures to the *hands* through their presenting question. Can Christians smoke pot? No. Don't *do* it.

Practicing the Method Until It Becomes Second Nature

Children learning to communicate don't focus on the steps for long. They're not breaking down the components of effective communication in order to ask for some milk. No, these steps become so instinctive they emerge with astonishing ease.

In the same way, Breeden and Ward model the skills of OIA Bible study without drawing attention to those skills. Thus it may have felt tedious to some readers as I listed examples of each of the steps, above.

But if you'd like to understand your Bible, you likewise must be able to use it to answer your questions. And the best way to do that is to practice these skills repeatedly until they become second-nature. The more you practice, the easier it will be to catch the Bible's ideas without getting overwhelmed by all the words on the page.

And let me end this appendix with a simple caution. As you observe, interpret, and apply, the most important thing is always to do so *in context*. Read each verse in the context of the chapter, each chapter in the context of the section, each section in the context of the book, and each book in the context of the Bible. Context makes all the difference.

Take, for example, a single statement that might be made by two individuals. One wears an apron and chef's hat, with finger pointed at a wide metal rack in a noisy commercial kitchen. Another has a dreamy look in his eyes, with a funky, smoky smell wafting from his tie-dyed muscle shirt. Observing the context makes all the difference in both your interpretation and your resulting application, as you hear each speaker remark: "That pot is off the hook."

Observe, interpret, and apply. Do this well, and you'll be able to use the Bible to answer your questions.

Peter Krol is president of DiscipleMakers campus ministry. He blogs at KnowableWord.com, where he helps ordinary people learn to study the Bible.

Endnotes

1. *Westminster Confession of Faith*, 1.6
2. As discussed later in this chapter, "new creation" in the broad sense is a process that culminates in the return of Jesus. Some Christians do believe that at Jesus' Second Coming, God will *replace* the earth and heavens with completely new ones. While that issue is outside the scope of his book, the authors understand that on that day the new heavens and new earth will be "new" in the same way the resurrected body of Jesus was new, *without* his earthly body having been discarded—and that the bodies of Christians in their eternal state will be spiritually "new" in the same way.
3. Albert Wolters, *Creation Regained: Biblical Basics for a Reformational Worldview*, 2nd. ed. (Grand Rapids: Eerdmans, 2005), 46–47.
4. John Frame, *Systematic Theology*, (Phillipsburg, NJ: P&R Publishing Co., 2013), 191.
5. Biblical theology is studying each book of the Bible or passage of Scripture in the context of the whole Bible. Rather than just gathering as many verses as we can, biblical theology aims to understand those verses in the context of the Bible's narrative of creation, fall, redemption, and consummation. This book is a small sample of that kind of theology. If this is a new idea for you, the appendix in this book will flesh it out for you more.
6. *Cannabis sativa* is one of the main types of marijuana cultivated for its pyschoactive properties (the other being *cannabis indica*), though it can be used for hemp as well.
7. We're not saying this is always easy. We're saying that the difficulty doesn't eliminate the obligation.
8. Wayne Grudem, *Politics According to the Bible*. (Grand Rapids: Zondervan, 2010), 78. Emphasis in original.
9. "Common grace" refers to the manifestations of God's grace and mercy that he bestows on all people and all creation—the good things we share in common.
10. Douglas J. Moo, *The Epistle to the Romans*. (Grand Rapids: William B. Eerdmans Publishing Co., 1996), 797.
11. The question of the proper scope of states' rights under the U.S. Constitution is not under consideration in this book. The fact remains, however, that as of this writing the federal government would be legally justified in arresting recreational users of marijuana in any state.

12. Martin Lee, *Smoke Signals: A Social History of Marijuana– Medical, Recreational and Scientific* (NewYork: Scribner, 2013).
13. Edward J.Young, *The Book of Isaiah, Volume 2*, (Grand Rapids: William B. Eerdmans Publishing Co., 1969), 529.
14. William Hendriksen, *Luke*, (Grand Rapids: Baker Books, 1978), 595.
15. Lee, *ibid*.
16. John Frame, *Doctrine of the Christian Life* (Phillipsburg, NJ: P&R, 2008).
17. Timothy Keller, *The Reason for God Discussion Guide: Conversations on Faith and Life* (Grand Rapids: Zondervan, 2010), 56.
18. Frame writes, "In general, the biblical principles governing alcohol pertain to drugs as well. In some cases (such as medical marijuana and many prescription drugs), there are benefits to be gained, and those benefits should be received with thanks. (I do not believe, for example, that the medicinal use of marijuana should be outlawed.) As we have seen with alcohol, Scripture also approves of a certain level of mood alteration in situations where one does not have to give close attention to one's environment. But the biblical writers who counsel against addiction to alcohol would certainly also disapprove of addiction to heroin and cocaine.The principles are no different, but the danger of addiction is much greater. So to use such highly addictive substances is not biblically wise." *The Doctrine of the Christian Life* (pp. 741–742).
19. See Blomberg, Craig L., *Jesus and the Gospels*, (Nashville: B&H Academic, 2009), 262 and Keener, Craig S., *The Gospel of John, Volume One*, (Peabody: Hendrickson Publishers, 2010), 500-501.
20. DouglasWilson, "Two Birds with One Stoner," *Blog and Mablog* (blog), June 11, 2016, https://dougwils.com/the-church/two-birds-one-stoner.html. Accessed 08/14/2016.
21. National HighwayTraffic Safety Administration, "Cannabis/ Marijuana," http://www.nhtsa.gov/people/injury/research/job-185drugs/cannabis.htm, Accessed 9/4/2015.
22. John Patton at CovenantTheological Seminary summarizes this line of thinking well. He concludes that, "Much study has shown that although intoxication from alcohol results from immoderate or abusive use, even small to moderate amounts of marijuana can, except in rare circumstances, lead to intoxication.Thus, abstaining from marijuana use would seem to be consistent with biblical principles related to intoxication." https://issuu.com/covenantseminary/docs/fall_2014_vol29_1-2

23. http://www.cancerresearchuk.org/about-cancer/cancers-in-general/cancer-questions/does-smoking-cannabis-cause-cancer
24. https://en.wikipedia.org/wiki/Legality_of_cannabis U.S. states, too: http://norml.org/states.
25. Many thanks to http://www.equalrights4all.org/religious/bible.htm for this gem.
26. The instructive portions of the next three sections have been abridged from my book *Knowable Word: Helping Ordinary People Learn to Study the Bible*, Cruciform Press, 2014.

Knowable Word
Helping Ordinary People Learn to Study the Bible

by Peter Krol
Foreword by Tedd Tripp

Observe...Interpret...Apply

Simple concepts at the heart of good Bible study. Learn the basics in a few minutes—gain skills for a lifetime. The spiritual payoff is huge...ready?

108 pages   *bit.ly/Knowable*

"Peter Krol has done us a great service by writing the book Knowable Word. It is valuable for those who have never done in-depth Bible study and a good review for those who have. I look forward to using this book to improve my own Bible study."
Jerry Bridges, author, The Pursuit of Holiness, and many more

"It is hard to over-estimate the value of this tidy volume. It is clear and uncomplicated. No one will be off-put by this book. It will engage the novice and the serious student of Scripture. It works as a solid read for individuals or as an exciting study for a small group."
Tedd Tripp, pastor and author (from the Foreword)

"At the heart of *Knowable Word* is a glorious and crucial conviction: that understanding the Bible is not the preserve of a few, but the privilege and joy of all God's people. Peter Krol's book demystifies the process of reading God's Word and in so doing enfranchises the people of God. I warmly encourage you to read it.."
Dr. Tim Chester, The Porterbrook Network

"Here is an excellent practical guide to interpreting the Bible. Krol has thought through, tested, and illustrated in a clear, accessible way basic steps in interpreting the Bible, and made everything available in a way that will encourage ordinary people to deepen their own study."
Vern Poythress, Westminster Theological Seminary

Does God Listen to Rap?
Christians and the World's Most Controversial Music

by Curtis "Voice" Allen

How can Christians think biblically about art forms that have sinful roots? This Reformed Rap pioneer offers a fascinating history of the development of rap, tells his own story, and unpacks some vital Scripture passages about faith and the arts.

bit.ly/God-Rap

"So long as we live Christ-honoring lives, speak of Christ to the lost, recognize the world-defying power of gospel witness in any form, and make music that does not compromise biblical teaching, we're free—joyfully, exuberantly free—to rap as we see fit. This book makes the case better than I can. You should dig into it. You'll learn much historically, you'll be blessed by Curt's scriptural and theological reflections, and you'll have fun doing it....Almost as much fun as I'm having watching the Lord use my brother as he speaks a prophetic word and blesses God's church through the use of his artistic and literary gifts."

Owen Strachan, Director, Center on Gospel and Culture,
Midwestern Baptist Theological Seminary

"A very sane and very good introduction to a much controverted subject....I have read a lot of cultural analysis, and Allen comes to the subject in fresh ways....this was a really valuable book, and I highly recommend it. I didn't find myself colliding with any of its basic assumptions on cultural engagement....Gifted Christian poets and lyricists should never be content with throwing their words down into the sinkhole of momentary culture. They should be aiming for something higher, and books like this help."

Douglas Wilson, author, pastor

Smooth Stones
Bringing Down the Giant
Questions of Apologetics

by Joe Coffey

Street-level apologetics for everyday Christians.

Because faith in Jesus makes sense. And you don't need an advanced degree to understand why.

101 pages   bit.ly/CPStones

"What a thrill for me to see Joe Coffey, a graduate of our first Centurions Program class, apply the biblical worldview principles we teach at BreakPoint and the Colson Center. In this marvelous little book, Joe simply and succinctly lays out the tenets of the Christian faith within the context of the four key life and worldview questions. This is an excellent resource for Christians and non-Christians alike who are seeking the Truth."

> ***Chuck Colson, Founder of Prison Fellowship and the Colson Center for Christian Worldview***

"This book may be the best resource I've seen to answer common objections in everyday language."

> ***Jared Totten, Critical Thinking Blog***

"A quick read that packs a punch.... I'm always on the lookout for something like this. *Smooth Stones* is a winner."

> ***Mike del Rosario, ApologeticsGuy.Com***

"Most books on apologetics are too long, too deep, and too complicated. This book has none of these defects. Like its title, it is like a smooth stone from David's apologetic sling directed right to the mind of an enquiring reader"

> ***Norman L. Geisler, Distinguished Professor of Apologetics, Veritas Evangelical Seminary, Murrieta, CA***

Do Ask, Do Tell, Let's Talk
Why and How Christians Should Have Gay Friends

by Brad Hambrick

Conversations among friends accomplish more than debates between opponents.

118 pages
bit.ly/ASKTELL

""This is a book the church has desperately needed for some time. It is simply excellent. It will challenge you and guide you in navigating in a more Christlike manner the host of questions surrounding same-sex attraction and the local church."
Danny Akin, Pres., Southeastern Baptist Theological Seminary

""To stand on what we believe is clear in Scripture, and to be a friend, at the same time – this book is an important next step for Christian literature on same-sex attraction. It doesn't simply guide us in wise engagement; it guides us in friendships where there is mutual enjoyment and appreciation. And Brad does this in such a way that he doesn't cut any theological corners but makes such friendships a necessary expression of our theology."
Ed Welch, counselor and faculty member, Christian Counseling and Educational Foundation

""Whenever Jesus encountered a sexual minority, he responded with love and friendship instead of shame. Brad Hambrick helps us see how we, too, can create safe space and belonging for our LGBTQ friends. Why? So that these friends, too, can encounter the grace and truth of Jesus. I highly recommend this book."
Scott Sauls, pastor, Christ Presbyterian Church, Nashville

CPSIA information can be obtained
at www.ICGtesting.com
Printed in the USA
LVOW04s1519081016
507901LV00005B/7/P